The AI Assisted Author: Harnessing Technology to Elevate Your Writing

Written By Rob Watts with the creative assistance of AI

For Albie with Love

Introduction

Welcome to "The AI Assisted Author: Harnessing Technology to Elevate Your Writing." Whether you're a seasoned writer, an aspiring novelist, or simply someone curious about the evolving landscape of storytelling, this book is for you.

In a world where technology is rapidly transforming how we create and consume content, the fusion of Artificial Intelligence (AI) with the art of writing presents both an exciting opportunity and a an array of challenges.

Who is this book for?

This book is designed for anyone who has ever faced the daunting task of staring at a blank page, unsure of how to begin or where to take their story next.

It's for those who want to enhance their creative process, streamline their workflow, and explore new ways of storytelling through the power of AI.

Whether you're a writer looking to overcome writer's block, an editor aiming to polish a manuscript, or simply a creative mind eager to experiment with new tools, this book offers valuable insights and practical guidance.

What can you expect from this book?

In "The AI Assisted Author," you'll find a comprehensive guide that walks you through the entire writing process with AI as your collaborator.

From the initial stages of brainstorming and planning your book, to drafting, editing, and finally publishing, this book will show you how to harness AI technology to elevate your writing.

You'll discover how AI can assist in generating ideas, refining prose, and even suggesting plot twists you might not have considered.

Each chapter is filled with step-by-step instructions, real-world examples, and exercises designed to help you integrate AI into your creative process seamlessly. **What will you learn?**

Throughout this book, you will learn how to:

- **Understand AI's capabilities and limitations**: Grasp the basics of how AI works in the context of writing, and learn to use its strengths while navigating its weaknesses.

- **Plan your book with AI assistance**: Use AI tools to brainstorm ideas, outline your narrative, and structure your chapters, ensuring a well-organised and compelling story.

- **Write your first draft in collaboration with AI**: Engage in a collaborative process where AI helps you craft authentic dialogue, vivid scenes, and complex characters while maintaining your unique voice.

- **Edit and refine with AI**: Learn how to leverage AI tools to enhance clarity, coherence, and style, all while preserving the emotional depth and creativity that define your work.

- **Overcome challenges and ethical considerations**: Address common concerns about using AI in writing, such as maintaining originality, navigating ethical dilemmas, and ensuring that your creative voice remains at the forefront.

- **Innovate and explore new creative possibilities**: Push the boundaries of traditional storytelling by experimenting with new genres, styles, and narrative techniques made possible by AI.

- **Publishing:** Discover how and where to get published, along with the things to consider when doing so.

As you embark on this journey, "The AI Author" will be your guide, helping you unlock the full potential of AI in your writing.

The world of storytelling is evolving, and with the right tools and knowledge, you can stay ahead of the curve and create stories that resonate deeply with your readers. So, whether you're here to streamline your writing process, explore new creative frontiers, or simply enhance your skills, this book will provide the insights and tools you need to succeed in the era of AI-assisted writing.

Goals of the Book

- **Empowering Writers**: *The primary goal of this book is to empower you by providing the knowledge and tools to effectively use AI in your writing process. The book aims to demystify AI, making it accessible to writers of all levels, including you.*

- **Practical Guidance**: *This book offers practical, hands-on guidance. It's not just about theory; it's about how you can immediately start using AI tools to enhance your writing. This includes step-by-step instructions, case studies, and exercises designed to help you integrate AI into your creative process.*

- **Balancing AI with Human Creativity**: *This book offers strategies for maintaining the human element in your writing while leveraging the strengths of AI, ensuring that your voice remains central.*

- **Encouraging Innovation**: *You will be encouraged to experiment with AI in your writing, pushing the boundaries of what's possible. This book aims to inspire you to think of AI not as a threat, but as a tool that can open up new creative possibilities and enhance your storytelling.*

- **Exploring Ethical Implications**: *Finally, the book will explore the ethical considerations of using AI in writing. This includes discussions on authorship, originality, and the potential biases inherent in AI-generated content. The goal is to provide you with a balanced view that respects both the potential and limitations of AI in the creative process.*

Chapter 1

The Intersection of Writing and AI

Picture yourself sitting down at your desk, a cup of coffee in hand, ready to work on your latest novel. The cursor blinks on an empty screen, a daunting reminder of the chapter that needs to be written. But instead of facing this challenge alone, you open up an AI-powered writing tool. Within seconds, you've brainstormed new ideas, received feedback on your last chapter, and even generated a few sentences to kickstart your creativity. This isn't a scene from a distant future—it's the reality of writing with AI today.

But how did we get here? It's useful to look at how AI has evolved over time, how its role in modern writing is changing the way creators create and how it's bridging technology and creativity like never before..

The Evolution of AI in Creativity

The evolution of artificial intelligence (AI) has been a remarkable journey, starting from basic algorithms to the advanced models capable of generating text, art, and music today.

The story of AI begins in the mid-20th century with the development of simple algorithms designed to perform specific tasks, such as the earliest chess-playing programs.

These early efforts were based on rule-based systems, where a set of predefined rules determined the output. While impressive for their time, these systems lacked the ability to learn or adapt, limiting their capabilities.

The introduction of machine learning in the 1980s marked a significant turning point. Rather than relying solely on predefined rules, machine learning allowed computers to learn from data and improve over time.

This era saw the development of neural networks, inspired by the human brain's structure, though their potential was initially limited by computational constraints.

A major breakthrough came in the 2000s with the advent of deep learning, a subset of machine learning that uses multi-layered neural networks to process vast amounts of data. This led to dramatic improvements in tasks such as image and speech recognition. Around this time, AI began to make its mark on creative fields, with systems capable of composing music, generating poetry, and even creating visual art. However, these early creative endeavours were often rudimentary and lacked the nuanced understanding of context and style that human creators possess.

The development of the GPT (Generative Pre-trained Transformer) models by OpenAI represents a landmark in AI's evolution. The first model, GPT, was introduced in 2018, followed by GPT-2 in 2019, and GPT-3 in 2020. These models utilised transformers, a type of neural network architecture that excels at understanding and generating human-like text by processing and learning from large datasets of text from the internet. GPT-3, in particular, demonstrated an unprecedented ability to generate coherent, contextually appropriate, and creative text, often indistinguishable from human writing.

These advancements have had a profound impact on creative fields, especially writing. AI-driven tools like GPT models have enabled writers to brainstorm ideas, generate content, and even co-author works. They have democratised access to high-quality content creation, allowing individuals and small businesses to produce professional-grade writing without extensive resources. However, they have also sparked debates about authorship, originality, and the role of AI in creative processes.

In visual arts and music, AI has pushed boundaries, creating original compositions and artworks that challenge traditional notions of creativity. AI-generated art has been sold at major auction houses, and AI-composed music is being explored in various genres. As AI continues to evolve, its role in creative fields will likely expand, offering new possibilities and raising new questions about the nature of creativity itself. The journey from simple algorithms to today's sophisticated models reflects AI's growing influence and its potential to reshape the creative landscape.

AI's Role in Modern Writing

AI has transitioned from a novelty in the writing world to a powerful, widely embraced tool that is reshaping how writers approach their craft. Initially viewed as a curiosity, AI's capabilities have matured to the point where it now plays a significant role in various stages of the writing process, from brainstorming and idea generation to providing instant feedback and even co-authoring books.

One of the most prominent applications of AI in writing is its ability to assist with idea generation. Tools like Sudowrite and ChatGPT allow writers to quickly explore different plotlines, character developments, and themes by generating suggestions based on brief prompts. This capability can help overcome writer's block, offering fresh perspectives that might not have been considered otherwise.

AI also excels at providing instant feedback, a feature that has become invaluable for both new and experienced writers. Grammarly, for example, uses AI to analyse text for grammar, style, and tone, offering real-time suggestions that help improve the clarity and effectiveness of the writing. This immediate feedback loop enables writers to refine their work continuously, making the editing process more efficient.

Beyond assistance and feedback, AI has even taken on the role of a co-author. A notable example is the novel "1 the Road," written by AI in collaboration with author Ross Goodwin. The AI system generated text based on inputs from various sensors during a road trip, contributing to a unique and experimental narrative. Another example is the poetry collection "The Sunlight Press," where AI was used to generate some of the poems alongside human poets.

These examples illustrate how AI is becoming an integral part of the writing community, not just as a tool for assistance but as a creative partner. As AI continues to advance, its influence on the writing process is likely to grow, offering new possibilities and challenging traditional notions of authorship and creativity. This shift reflects a broader trend in the creative industries, where AI is increasingly seen as a valuable collaborator rather than just a technological novelty.

Bridging Technology and Creativity

AI acts as a powerful bridge between the logical world of technology and the imaginative realm of creativity, forging a symbiotic relationship that enhances the creative process in unprecedented ways. This intersection of logic and creativity *represents one of the most exciting developments in both fields, where the strengths of each are amplified by the other.*

On the technological side, AI excels at processing vast amounts of data, identifying patterns, and providing structured suggestions. It brings a level of precision, efficiency, and consistency that can be challenging to achieve through human effort alone.

For instance, AI can analyse a body of text and offer improvements in grammar, style, and structure, ensuring that the technical aspects of writing are polished. Tools like AI-driven content generators can suggest plot developments, character arcs, or thematic elements based on extensive databases of literature, allowing writers to explore new ideas and directions that they might not have considered otherwise.

However, while AI can provide structure, it is the human touch that infuses creativity with emotion, depth, and originality. Creativity thrives on the unpredictable, the emotional, and the deeply personal—qualities that AI, despite its advancements, cannot replicate. Writers and artists use AI-generated suggestions as a springboard, taking those logical outputs and transforming them with their unique perspectives, experiences, and imagination. The result is work that is both technically sound and richly infused with human emotion and creativity.

This collaboration between AI and human creativity is not about one replacing the other but rather about enhancing what each brings to the table. AI provides the scaffolding—the structure and suggestions—upon which human creativity can build something truly original and profound. In this way, AI serves as a catalyst for creativity, enabling artists and writers to push the boundaries of their craft, explore new genres, and experiment with innovative forms of expression.

As AI continues to evolve, this bridge between technology and creativity will likely become even more robust, offering new tools and possibilities for creative professionals. The ongoing dialogue between the logical and imaginative realms will shape the future of creative industries, leading to a new era of collaboration where technology and creativity are not at odds but are partners in innovation.

Why Write a Book with AI?

Purists may balk at the idea of using AI to write or create content, but the reality is that creators have always drawn upon the works and labours of others across various forms and genres throughout history. This practice of building upon existing material is not new; it has been a cornerstone of creativity for centuries.

In literature, figures like William Shakespeare famously drew heavily from earlier plays, historical texts, and classical mythology to craft his iconic works.

Similarly, the Roman poet Virgil's "Aeneid" was inspired by Homer's "Iliad" and "Odyssey," weaving familiar themes into a new narrative that reflected Roman ideals. In the visual arts, Renaissance masters frequently referenced classical sculptures and paintings, reinterpreting them within their cultural context.

For instance, Michelangelo's David was influenced by earlier depictions of the biblical figure but was infused with Renaissance humanism, illustrating how past and present intertwine in artistic creation.

In music, composers like Johann Sebastian Bach adapted and transformed existing musical forms and motifs, demonstrating how synthesis and reinterpretation have long driven creative innovation.

Before the digital age, creators relied on traditional methods to gather inspiration and knowledge. Libraries served as the primary repositories of information, where writers and scholars would spend countless hours poring over books, manuscripts, and periodicals to inform their work. Oral traditions, including stories, myths, and folklore, were passed down through generations, influencing literary and artistic creations.

Visual references, such as paintings, sculptures, and architectural works, provided a rich source of inspiration for artists who studied these pieces to learn techniques and styles. While these methods were more labour-intensive than today's AI tools, they laid the foundation for the intertextual and interdisciplinary practices that continue to shape creative work today.

The evolution from these traditional methods to the use of AI reflects a continuous thread in the creative process: the blending of existing knowledge with new insights to produce something original, referencing the collective endeavours of mankind.

The Practical And Creative Benefits Of Using AI

- **Efficiency and Speed**: *One of the most compelling reasons for you to use AI in writing is the speed and efficiency it offers. AI can streamline your writing process, from brainstorming to drafting and editing, allowing you to produce content faster and with greater ease.*

- **Overcoming Writer's Block**: *AI can be a powerful tool for overcoming writer's block. Whether you need to generate new ideas, gain fresh perspectives, or find starting points for scenes and dialogue, AI can help you push through creative barriers and keep your writing flowing.*

- **Enhancing Creativity**: *Contrary to the belief that AI might stifle creativity, it can actually enhance it by offering suggestions and generating content that might inspire new directions in your story. AI can serve as a creative partner, encouraging you to explore new genres, styles, or narrative techniques that you might not have considered otherwise.*

- **Access to Advanced Tools**: *AI also democratises access to advanced writing tools that were once only available to those with significant resources. These tools include editing software, research tools, and platforms that assist with everything from plot development to marketing strategies, making sophisticated writing tools more accessible to all.*

- **Exploring New Forms of Collaboration**: *Writing with AI is not about replacing the human author, but about a new form of collaboration. This partnership can lead to innovative storytelling approaches and the exploration of new genres or formats, opening up creative possibilities you may not have previously imagined.*

Chapter 2

Understanding AI and Its Capabilities

As you start exploring the world of AI-assisted writing, you realise that AI is already part of your everyday life — from the virtual assistants that answer your questions to the recommendation algorithms that suggest your next favourite book.

You begin to see how these AI systems, trained in language processing and content generation, can be powerful allies in your writing journey.

With AI tools like GPT models, you can brainstorm new ideas, refine your prose, and even get instant feedback on your drafts. Understanding AI's strengths and limitations helps you harness its capabilities while keeping your creative vision front and centre.

What is AI?

Artificial Intelligence (AI) is a field of computer science that focuses on creating systems capable of performing tasks that traditionally require human intelligence.

These tasks include a wide range of cognitive functions, such as understanding and processing natural language, recognising patterns, learning from experience, and making informed decisions. AI systems are designed to mimic human cognitive abilities, allowing them to interact with the world in ways that were once the sole domain of humans.

At its core, AI encompasses several subfields, each contributing to the overall goal of developing intelligent machines.

Machine learning, for instance, is a key aspect of AI that involves training algorithms to recognise patterns and make predictions based on data. This enables AI systems to learn and improve over time without being explicitly programmed for every possible scenario. Another crucial component is natural language processing (NLP), which allows AI to understand, interpret, and generate human language, facilitating communication between humans and machines.

In the context of writing, AI's capabilities can be harnessed in various ways. Natural language processing enables AI to analyse text, understand context, and generate content that is coherent and contextually relevant.

For example, AI can assist in generating creative ideas, drafting articles, or even completing entire sections of a manuscript. It can also provide real-time feedback on grammar, style, and tone, helping writers refine their work more efficiently.

Moreover, AI's ability to recognise patterns can be applied to large datasets of text, allowing it to identify trends, summarise information, and offer insights that can inform a writer's approach. This can be particularly useful in research-heavy writing projects, where AI can sift through vast amounts of information to extract relevant data.

By grasping these basics of AI—understanding its capabilities in natural language processing, pattern recognition, and decision-making—you can begin to see how AI can be a powerful tool in the writing process.

It acts as a collaborator that can augment your creativity, streamline your workflow, and enhance the quality of your writing, ultimately allowing you to focus more on the imaginative aspects of your work.

The Role of AI in Language Processing:

AI plays a crucial role in language processing, particularly through the field of Natural Language Processing (NLP), which is the branch of AI that focuses on enabling computers to understand, interpret, and generate human language. NLP is at the heart of many AI-driven applications, from simple chatbots to complex content generation systems, and is fundamental to how AI can assist in writing.

At its most basic level, NLP involves the analysis and manipulation of human language data. This can include tasks such as parsing sentences to understand grammatical structures, extracting meaning from text, and even translating languages. AI models that utilize NLP are trained on vast datasets of text, allowing them to learn the nuances of language—its syntax, semantics, and contextual subtleties. As these models become more sophisticated, they gain the ability to perform more complex tasks that are incredibly useful in writing.

One key application of AI in language processing is text generation. AI models like GPT (Generative Pre-trained Transformer) can produce coherent and contextually appropriate text based on a given prompt. These models analyse the input, understand the context, and generate text that can range from completing sentences to drafting entire articles. This capability can be a powerful tool for writers, providing them with drafts, ideas, or even fully developed passages that can serve as a foundation for further development.

Another critical aspect of NLP is text analysis, where AI can read and comprehend large amounts of text quickly. This is particularly useful in research and editing. AI can summarise articles, extract key points, and even analyze sentiment and tone. For instance, when editing, AI can detect inconsistencies in style or tone across a manuscript, helping writers maintain a consistent voice. Additionally, AI-powered grammar checkers and style guides can provide real-time feedback, suggesting improvements in clarity, conciseness, and correctness.

Furthermore, AI in NLP is also used in translation, where it can convert text from one language to another with increasing accuracy. This capability allows writers to reach a broader audience by translating their work into multiple languages, while still maintaining the original meaning and tone.

Understanding these capabilities of AI in language processing helps to illuminate how AI can be an invaluable partner in the writing process. It goes beyond mere automation, offering insights, suggestions, and enhancements that can elevate the quality of writing. Whether you're brainstorming ideas, drafting content, editing for precision, or translating your work, AI's ability to process and generate language can significantly augment your creative process, making it faster, more efficient, and potentially more innovative.

AI in Everyday Life:

AI has seamlessly integrated into many aspects of our daily lives, often in ways we might not immediately recognise. By understanding these everyday applications of AI, the idea of using it in more specialised tasks like writing becomes more familiar and approachable.

One of the most common examples of AI in daily life is through virtual assistants like Siri, Alexa, and Google Assistant. These AI-powered tools help us perform a variety of tasks, from setting reminders and sending messages to controlling smart home devices and answering trivia questions. They rely on Natural Language Processing (NLP) to understand spoken language, interpret commands, and provide accurate, context-sensitive responses. This interaction with AI has become so routine that many of us now rely on these virtual assistants to manage our day-to-day activities efficiently.

AI also plays a significant role in how we consume content. Recommendation algorithms on platforms like Netflix, Spotify, and YouTube analyse our viewing, listening, and browsing habits to suggest movies, shows, music, and videos that align with our preferences. These algorithms are powered by AI, which processes vast amounts of data to predict what we might enjoy based on our past behaviour. This personalised experience is another example of AI working behind the scenes to make our lives more convenient and tailored to our tastes.

In addition, AI is at work in the apps and tools we use for shopping, social media, and even email. For instance, AI-driven email filters help sort out spam, prioritise important messages, and suggest responses through predictive text. On social media platforms like Facebook and Instagram, AI algorithms curate our feeds, deciding which posts we see based on our interactions and preferences.

Recognising these everyday uses of AI helps demystify the technology and illustrates how it can be a natural extension of our existing digital habits. Just as AI enhances our entertainment choices, manages our schedules, and tailors our online experiences, it can also be a valuable tool in writing. Whether through generating ideas, improving grammar, or suggesting content structures, AI in writing is simply another way this technology can enhance our lives, making tasks more efficient and enjoyable. Understanding this continuity helps make the concept of AI in writing feel *less like a futuristic leap and more like a logical progression of the tools we already use every day.*

Types of AI for Writing

- ***Large Language Models (LLM's)****: LLM's, such as GPT, which are designed to generate text based on input prompts. These models are trained on vast amounts of text, enabling them to predict and generate coherent, contextually appropriate text. This is the type of AI that can assist you in generating content for your writing projects.*

- ***Content Generation Tools****: There are a variety of AI content generation tools available to you as a writer. These tools can help you generate articles, blog posts, short stories, and even poetry. Knowing about tools like OpenAI's GPT-based platforms, Jasper, and Copy.ai can open up new possibilities for your writing process.*

- ***Editing and Proofreading Aids****:AI-driven editing tools such as Grammarly, Hemingway Editor, and ProWritingAid go beyond basic spell-checking—they analyse your grammar, style, tone, and readability, helping you improve the overall quality of your work. These tools can become invaluable as you refine your drafts.*

- ***AI for Research****: AI can help you gather information quickly and organise it efficiently. AI-based search engines and data analysis platforms can make your research phase more streamlined, allowing you to focus on the creative aspects of your writing.*

Strengths and Limitations of AI

- *AI's Strengths:*

  - **Efficiency and Speed**: *AI can process large amounts of data and generate text much faster than you might be able to do manually. This efficiency can be a huge asset, especially when you need to produce content quickly or handle repetitive writing tasks.*

  - **Consistency and Objectivity**: *AI provides consistent output without the biases, fatigue, or emotional influences that might affect your writing. This can be particularly useful in tasks requiring uniformity, such as technical writing or content creation at scale.*

  - **Inspiration and Idea Generation**: *AI as a creative catalyst offers new perspectives or suggestions that you might not have considered. This can be especially helpful when you're brainstorming or trying to overcome writer's block.*

- *AI's Limitations:*

  - **Lack of True Understanding**: *AI, despite its capabilities, does not truly comprehend the content it generates. It can produce text that appears meaningful but may lack depth, nuance, or contextual appropriateness, particularly in complex or emotionally charged topics.*

  - **Creativity and Originality**: *Recognise that while AI can generate content, it is limited to recombining existing ideas and patterns found in its training data. It cannot create truly original content in the way that your human mind can, particularly in areas requiring deep creativity and innovation.*

  - **Ethical and Bias Concerns**: *Be aware that AI systems can unintentionally perpetuate biases present in their training data, leading to output that may reflect societal prejudices. Additionally, the use of AI raises questions about authorship and originality, particularly when AI-generated content closely mimics human writing.*

Chapter 3

Planning and Researching Your Book with AI

Ok, so you're about to start planning a new novel, and you want to make the most of AI's capabilities.

You begin by using an AI tool to brainstorm ideas, inputting a few basic concepts and receive a flood of creative possibilities in return. As you explore these ideas, AI suggests plot points that could work well in a genre you've never tried before — fantasy. Intrigued, you decide to outline the story with AI's help.

The AI assists you in breaking down the plot into chapters, ensuring that your pacing is spot-on and that each subplot is woven seamlessly into the main narrative. With AI's support, your research is also more efficient, as the AI helps you gather and organise all the background information you need.

By the time you're ready to start writing, you have a clear plan and all the tools you need to bring your story to life.

Let's look at a few of those processes in more detail.

Brainstorming Ideas

Using AI to Generate Concepts: *When you're starting a new writing project, AI can be a powerful tool for brainstorming ideas. By inputting basic concepts or themes into an AI tool, you can generate a wide range of story ideas and scenarios to explore. This can be especially useful if you're feeling stuck or need a fresh perspective to kickstart your creativity.*

Exploring Different Genres: *AI can also help you experiment with different genres by offering suggestions that might push you out of your comfort zone. For instance, if you usually write crime fiction, AI might inspire you to explore fantasy or science fiction, helping you expand your creative horizons.*

Developing Themes and Motifs: *Use AI to help identify and develop themes and motifs within your book. By providing the AI with your initial ideas, you can receive suggestions on how to weave these themes consistently throughout your narrative, ensuring that your story is cohesive and compelling.*

Imagine you're a writer embarking on a new novel, but you're struggling to come up with a compelling premise. You decide to use an AI tool to help generate ideas.

You input a few basic concepts: "a small town," "a mysterious stranger," and "a hidden secret." The AI responds with several intriguing scenarios:

1. **A small coastal town is visited by a stranger who claims to be from the future, warning the townspeople of an impending disaster tied to a long-buried artifact.**

2. **In a remote village, a stranger arrives, and his presence begins to unravel the town's dark history, revealing a secret society that has controlled the town's fate for generations.**

3. **A traveler stumbles upon a small town where everyone seems to have forgotten their past, and only the mysterious stranger holds the key to their memories.**

These AI-generated ideas spark your imagination, helping you to envision a unique plot line that blends elements of mystery and suspense.

Next, you decide to push yourself creatively by exploring different genres. Typically, you write crime fiction, but you're curious about branching into something new. You input the scenario, "a detective searching for a missing person," into the AI and ask it to reimagine this premise in different genres. The AI suggests:

1.In a fantasy setting, the detective is a rogue sorcerer searching for a missing princess in a kingdom where magic is outlawed.

2.In a science fiction world, the detective is an AI sentient being tasked with finding a human who has gone missing in a space colony on the brink of rebellion.

3.In a historical drama, the detective is an exiled knight searching for his missing lord during the turbulent times of medieval Europe.

These genre-bending ideas inspire you to consider blending your love for crime fiction with elements of fantasy or science fiction, pushing you out of your comfort zone and opening up new creative possibilities.

Finally, as you begin outlining your novel, you use AI to help develop and weave themes and motifs throughout your narrative. You input your core themes—"betrayal," "redemption," and "identity"—and the AI suggests ways to reinforce these themes in your story. For example, it might suggest that the hidden artefact in the small town serves as a metaphor for the buried secrets of the townspeople, or that the mysterious stranger's quest for redemption mirrors the protagonist's journey to uncover the truth about their own identity. These suggestions help you create a more cohesive and thematically rich narrative.

Through this process, AI has not only helped you brainstorm ideas but also guided you in exploring new genres and deepening the thematic elements of your story, ultimately leading to a more compelling and original novel.

Outlining with AI

Creating a Structured Outline: AI can assist you in creating a detailed outline for your book, helping to organise your ideas logically and ensuring that your narrative flows smoothly. By inputting key plot points, character arcs, or major events, the AI can generate a structured outline that breaks down your story into manageable sections.

Chapter Breakdown and Key Points: AI can help you break down your chapters and identify key points, offering suggestions for pacing and the placement of crucial plot elements. This includes determining where to introduce new characters, when to reveal important information, or how to build tension leading up to a climax.

Balancing Subplots: If your book includes multiple subplots, AI can help you manage them effectively by ensuring they are well-integrated into the main storyline. The AI can suggest ways to interweave subplots so that they complement, rather than overshadow, the central narrative.

Research Assistance

Efficient Information Gathering: AI can streamline your research process by quickly sifting through large amounts of data to extract relevant information. This is particularly useful if you're writing a historical novel, technical content, or non-fiction, where accuracy and detail are essential

Organising Research Material: AI can help you categorise and organise your research materials, making it easier to access the information you need when you need it. For example, AI might help you organise notes by theme, character, or chronology, ensuring that your **research is structured and easy to navigate.**

AI-Generated Summaries: AI can generate summaries of complex research materials, making it easier for you to digest and apply the information. If you're working on a novel involving scientific elements, AI can summarise technical papers or articles, extracting key points to maintain accuracy without getting bogged down in jargon.

Chapter 4

Using AI In Your Writing

AI offers a multitude of ways of assisting your in your efforts. In this section, we will explore what these are and give examples of how they can assist you in your goals.

Collaborative Writing

Crafting Initial Prompts: *AI can be an invaluable collaborator from the outset and during the creative process, helping you get started and overcome the blank page syndrome. You can use AI to craft the initial prompts that kickstart your writing. By inputting a simple idea or concept, the AI generates text that you can build upon. For example, you might input a prompt like "Describe the first meeting between two rivals in a futuristic city" or "Write the opening scene of a historical romance set in 19th-century Paris." The AI will then generate a draft that you can refine and personalise, making it truly your own.*

Iterative Writing Process: *Think of AI as your writing partner in an iterative process. After generating an initial draft or scene, you can go back and revise the AI's output, adding your unique voice and style. This back-and-forth allows you to shape the narrative while benefiting from the AI's ability to generate content quickly. The key is to see AI as a tool that aids your creativity, not something that replaces it. You provide the direction, and the AI assists with generating and refining the content.*

Maintaining Control of the Narrative: *It's essential to maintain control over your narrative when using AI. While AI can generate dialogue, descriptions, or even plot points, it's up to you to decide which elements to keep and how to integrate them into your story. You can use AI to explore different narrative possibilities, but ultimately, the choices you make will define the direction and tone of your story. This approach ensures that your unique voice remains at the forefront of the creative process.*

Dialogue and Character Development

Crafting Authentic Dialogue*: AI can be a helpful tool in crafting dialogue that feels natural and engaging. You can input character descriptions, including their personality traits, background, and relationship dynamics, and ask the AI to generate dialogue that fits these parameters. For example, you might request dialogue between a gruff detective and a nervous informant or between two old friends reconnecting after years apart. AI-generated dialogue can serve as a starting point, giving you ideas that you can tweak and refine to better match your characters' voices.

Exploring Character Motivations*: Use AI to delve deeper into your characters' motivations. By providing context and background information, you can ask the AI to suggest how a character might react in a given situation or what might drive their actions. This can add layers of complexity to your characters, helping you develop more nuanced and believable personalities. AI can offer you alternative reactions or behaviours that you might not have considered, giving you new angles to explore in your story.

Creating Consistent Character Voices*: Consistency in character voices is crucial for maintaining a cohesive narrative. AI can assist you in ensuring that each character's dialogue remains true to their established personality throughout the story. By feeding the AI with examples of a character's speech patterns or typical phrases, you can generate dialogue that maintains consistency across different scenes or chapters. This ensures that your characters' voices are distinct and believable.

Scene Construction

Building Vivid Scenes*: AI can be a powerful tool in constructing detailed and immersive scenes. You can describe the basic elements of a scene—such as the setting, mood, and key actions—and let the AI generate a descriptive passage that brings the scene to life. For example, you might input a prompt like "Describe a bustling market in an ancient city" or "Write a tense confrontation between two characters on a stormy night." The AI will provide a foundation that you can then expand upon, adding your own details and flourishes to create a vivid, engaging scene.

Enhancing Atmosphere and Mood*: AI can also help you create the desired atmosphere for a scene by suggesting sensory details, such as sounds, smells, and textures, that enhance the reader's experience. If you want to evoke a sense of dread, you might prompt the AI with "Generate a description of an abandoned house at night, with creaking floorboards and the faint sound of wind howling through broken windows." The AI's output can serve as a starting point, which you can refine to heighten the mood and draw your readers deeper into the scene.

Pacing and Tension: Managing the pacing of your scenes is critical, especially in genres that require careful control of tension and suspense. AI can help you experiment with different levels of detail and sentence structure to influence the rhythm of your narrative. You can ask the AI to generate alternative versions of a scene with varying levels of intensity, allowing you to choose the one that best matches the pacing and tension you want to achieve. This iterative process can help you find the right balance between action and description, keeping your readers engaged from start to finish.

Balancing Creativity with AI Assistance

Maintaining Your Voice: When using AI, it's important to ensure that your unique voice remains prominent in the final draft. While AI can generate useful content, you should always review and revise it to match your style and tone. After the AI produces a draft, go through it and make adjustments that align with your vision, ensuring that the narrative flows naturally and authentically. This approach allows you to harness the efficiency of AI while preserving the creative elements that make your writing distinct.

Editing and Refining AI-Generated Text: Once you've used AI to generate a draft, it's crucial to thoroughly edit and refine the text. AI-generated content can sometimes be too generic or lack the depth and nuance you're aiming for. As you revise, focus on enhancing coherence, adding emotional depth, and ensuring stylistic consistency throughout the narrative. This step is where your creativity truly shines, as you shape the AI's output into a story that resonates with your readers.

Incorporating Feedback: Consider using AI as part of a feedback loop, where you generate text, refine it, and then use the AI again to review the revised draft. This iterative process can help you identify areas that need further development, ensuring that your final product is polished and well-crafted. By continuously incorporating feedback—both from AI and your own revisions—you can create a draft that is cohesive, engaging, and true to your original vision.

Chapter 5

Editing and Refining with AI

You've finally completed the first draft of your novel, and now it's time to refine it into a polished manuscript.

The thought of editing can be overwhelming, but you're not alone—AI tools are here to help.

You start by running your manuscript through Grammarly, which quickly flags hundreds of grammar and style issues. As you work through these suggestions, you find that most are helpful, but you're careful to preserve your unique voice, rejecting changes that feel too mechanical or out of sync with your style.

Next, you use ProWritingAid to enhance the clarity and coherence of your writing. The AI suggests rephrasing a particularly convoluted sentence, and after a few tweaks, it reads much more smoothly.

As you move on to refining your descriptions, you notice a scene that feels a bit flat. You ask the AI for suggestions and it proposes adding sensory details that transform the scene from ordinary to immersive. Each time you make a round of revisions, you run the text through the AI again, creating a feedback loop that helps you catch any remaining errors and refine your prose even further.

By the time you're finished, your manuscript is not only technically polished but also retains the emotional depth and creative flair that makes it uniquely yours.

Automated Editing Tools

Harnessing AI for Grammar and Style Checks: As you move into the editing phase, AI-driven editing tools can become your best ally.

Tools like Grammarly, ProWritingAid, and Hemingway Editor can quickly scan your writing for grammar mistakes, awkward phrasing, and stylistic inconsistencies. Instead of spending hours combing through your manuscript for errors, you can rely on AI to flag issues instantly, allowing you to focus on more significant revisions. However, remember to use these suggestions as a guide, not a rule—sometimes, your unique style might call for breaking the rules that AI tries to enforce.

Refining Tone and Voice: While using AI tools, it's crucial to maintain your unique voice. AI can suggest revisions that improve clarity or readability, but it's up to you to decide whether these changes align with your style. For instance, if the AI recommends simplifying a complex sentence, consider whether the revision enhances your message or if it dilutes the nuance you're aiming for. By selectively accepting AI's suggestions, you ensure that your manuscript remains true to your voice while benefiting from the tool's objectivity.

Content Refinement

Enhancing Clarity and Coherence: During the content refinement stage, AI can help you ensure that your writing is clear and coherent. Sometimes, your initial drafts might be full of ideas that flow quickly from your mind but aren't yet fully organised.

AI tools can help you identify areas where the text is unclear or where the ideas need to be reorganised. For example, if a paragraph feels muddled, AI might suggest splitting it into two or rephrasing certain parts to improve readability. You can then refine these suggestions to ensure they align with your overall narrative.

Improving Sentence Structure: AI is particularly useful for refining sentence structure. It can help you vary sentence length and complexity to improve the rhythm of your prose. If you tend to fall into repetitive patterns or use overly complex constructions, AI can offer alternative phrasings that are more engaging or easier to read.

By experimenting with these suggestions, you can enhance the readability of your manuscript while maintaining your personal style.

Elevating the Quality of Descriptions*: When it comes to descriptive writing, AI can assist you in enhancing the quality and vividness of your scenes.*

If a particular description feels flat or uninspired, AI can suggest additional details or more dynamic language. For instance, if you've described a sunset, AI might propose adding sensory details like the warm breeze or the colours reflecting off the water. These enhancements can make your scenes more immersive and engaging, drawing readers deeper into your narrative.

Feedback Loops

Creating a Continuous Improvement Cycle*: One of the most effective ways to refine your manuscript is through feedback loops, where you repeatedly use AI to review and improve your work.*

After making initial edits, run the text through an AI tool again to check for any remaining issues.

This iterative process allows you to catch errors you might have missed and ensure that each revision brings your manuscript closer to perfection. By consistently incorporating AI feedback, you create a cycle of continuous improvement that polishes your manuscript with each pass.

Using AI for Multiple Drafts*: As you work through multiple drafts of your manuscript, AI can help you maintain consistency and coherence.*

Each time you revise a draft, use AI to reassess the content, checking that your revisions align with the overall tone and structure of the book.

This process is particularly useful for maintaining narrative flow and ensuring that all elements of your story come together cohesively by the final draft.

Balancing AI Feedback with Human Insight*: While AI feedback is invaluable, it's important to balance it with your own intuition and creativity.*

AI can identify technical issues and suggest improvements, but only you can determine whether these changes enhance your story.

Always trust your instincts when it comes to narrative decisions, character development, and thematic elements.

By combining AI's analytical strengths with your creative insights, you can produce a manuscript that is both technically sound and deeply engaging.

Chapter 6

Overcoming Challenges in AI-Assisted Writing

You're working on a novel, and after a few hours of writing, you hit a wall.

The ideas aren't flowing as they did before, and you're tempted to let AI take over. While it's okay to use AI to help you push through a rough patch, it's important to remember that the story you're telling is uniquely yours.

You might use AI to generate a few ideas or suggest some dialogue, but then take those suggestions and mould them into something that resonates with your voice and style.

As you edit the AI-generated text, you notice that some phrases feel too generic or lack the emotional depth you're aiming for. So, you rewrite those sections, adding your personal touch.

In doing so, you ensure that the final draft is infused with your creativity, not just the AI's algorithms

Maintaining Creativity and Originality

Avoiding Over-Reliance on AI*: When using AI in your writing process, it's easy to become overly dependent on its suggestions and outputs. However, it's important to remember that AI is a tool, not a replacement for your creativity.*

To maintain originality, you should use AI as a starting point or a guide rather than letting it dictate your narrative.

For instance, if AI generates a passage that you like, take the time to personalise it—infuse your unique voice, add details that only you can envision, and ensure that the content aligns with your creative intentions.

After AI has helped you draft a section, go back and revise it with your own flair. Change the phrasing to match your voice, add unique metaphors, or include specific cultural references that resonate with your audience. By doing this, you'll ensure that the final product reflects your individual creativity, not just the AI's capabilities.

Using AI to Enhance, Not Replace, Your Ideas: Think of AI as a creative assistant that can help you explore new ideas, but don't let it replace your original concepts.

When AI suggests a plot twist or character development, take it as inspiration rather than a final solution.

Use the AI's ideas as a springboard for further brainstorming, and always aim to put your spin on the suggestions. This approach ensures that your work remains fresh and uniquely yours.

Ethical Considerations

Addressing Authorship and Ownership: One of the challenges you may face when using AI in your writing is the question of authorship.

Since AI is generating some of the content, it's essential to consider who truly owns the work.

Ethically, you should acknowledge the role of AI in your writing process, especially if it has contributed significantly to the text.

However, it's also important to recognise that your input—your ideas, creativity, and revisions—are what ultimately shape the final product.

If you're transparent about the AI's involvement and clear about your role as the primary author, you can navigate these ethical waters more confidently.

Managing AI Biases: AI models are trained on large datasets that reflect human language and behaviour, which means they can inadvertently perpetuate biases found in those data.

As a writer, it's your responsibility to critically evaluate the content AI produces, ensuring that it doesn't reinforce harmful stereotypes or biases.

When AI generates text, take the time to review it for any unintended bias. If you identify problematic content, revise it or use the AI's output as a basis for discussing and challenging those biases within your narrative. By doing so, you'll maintain ethical integrity in your writing.

Ensuring Originality and Avoiding Plagiarism: Another ethical challenge is ensuring that the content generated by AI is truly original and doesn't inadvertently mimic existing works too closely.

AI generates text based on patterns from its training data, which can sometimes result in content that is too similar to what's already out there.

To overcome this, you should always revise and adapt AI-generated content, adding your unique insights and perspectives.

Additionally, it's a good practice to run AI-generated text through plagiarism detection tools to ensure that your work is both original and ethical.

Avoiding AI Dependency

Balancing AI Assistance with Human Creativity: It's crucial to strike a balance between AI assistance and your own creativity. While AI can speed up the writing process and offer valuable suggestions, your work should always reflect your own thoughts and ideas.

Set clear boundaries for how and when you use AI in your writing process. For example, you might decide to use AI only for brainstorming or editing, leaving the core drafting process to your own creativity.

By setting these boundaries, you'll ensure that AI remains a tool in your toolkit rather than a crutch.

Building Confidence in Your Writing: Relying too heavily on AI can sometimes undermine your confidence in your own writing abilities. To avoid this, regularly challenge yourself to write without AI assistance.

Spend time honing your craft, practising different writing styles, and experimenting with new techniques.

The more you develop your skills, the less you'll feel the need to depend on AI, and the more confident you'll become in your ability to produce high-quality work on your own.

Chapter 7

Finalising and Publishing Your Book

You've put in countless hours writing and refining your book, and now you're ready to bring it to the world. But before you do, there are a few crucial steps to take.

You start by running your manuscript through an AI tool like Grammarly to catch any lingering errors and ensure that your writing is as polished as possible.

As you review the AI's suggestions, you're careful to maintain your unique voice, accepting changes that enhance clarity but rejecting those that alter your style.

Next, you consider your publishing options. You've always dreamed of seeing your book on the shelves of major bookstores, so you decide to pursue traditional publishing.

Using an AI tool, you research literary agents who specialise in your genre, and the AI helps you craft a compelling query letter that showcases the strengths of your book.

While waiting for responses, you also prepare for the possibility of self-publishing, using AI to design a professional cover and plan a marketing strategy that will help your book reach its target audience.

With AI's assistance, you feel confident that your book is ready for the world, whether you go the traditional route or take control of the publishing process yourself.

Polishing the Manuscript

Conducting a Final Review with AI*: As you approach the final stages of your manuscript, it's important to ensure that everything is polished and ready for publication.*

AI can be a valuable tool in conducting a thorough final review. Use AI-driven editing tools to scan your manuscript for any remaining grammar issues, inconsistencies, or awkward phrasing.

At this stage, the AI's suggestions can help you catch those last-minute errors that you might have missed in earlier drafts. However, be sure to maintain a critical eye—just because AI flags something doesn't necessarily mean it needs changing. Trust your instincts and make decisions that align with your overall vision for the book.

Refining Pacing and Flow*: One of the key aspects of a polished manuscript is the pacing and flow of the narrative.*

AI tools can assist by analysing the structure of your manuscript and offering suggestions on how to improve the pacing. For example, if a particular chapter feels too slow, AI might suggest trimming certain sections or combining scenes to maintain reader engagement.

You can use these insights to make adjustments that ensure your story unfolds smoothly and keeps readers hooked from start to finish.

Consistency Checks Across the Manuscript*: Consistency is crucial in a finished manuscript, whether it's maintaining the same tone, keeping character details uniform, or ensuring that plot points align correctly.*

AI can help you identify inconsistencies by comparing different sections of your manuscript. For instance, if a character's eye colour changes halfway through the book, AI might catch this discrepancy.

By conducting a final consistency check, you'll ensure that your manuscript is cohesive and professional.

Self-Publishing vs. Traditional Publishing

Understanding the Pros and Cons*: When it comes to publishing your book, one of the first decisions you'll need to make is whether to pursue self-publishing or traditional publishing.*

Each path has its advantages and challenges.

Self-publishing offers more control and faster turnaround times, but it also requires you to handle everything from marketing to cover design.

Traditional publishing, on the other hand, provides support from a publisher and access to established distribution channels, but it can be a longer and more competitive process.

AI can help you weigh the pros and cons by providing data-driven insights on market trends, reader preferences, and even financial projections.

Using AI to Streamline the Self-Publishing Process*: If you choose to self-publish, AI can simplify many aspects of the process. For example, AI tools can assist with formatting your manuscript for different platforms, ensuring that your book looks professional across all devices.*

Additionally, AI can help you design a cover that captures the essence of your book and appeals to your target audience.

You can input descriptions of your book's themes, tone, and genre, and the AI can generate cover design ideas or even create a finished product based on your input.

Navigating the Traditional Publishing Route with AI*: For those pursuing traditional publishing, AI can be a valuable ally in navigating the submission process.*

AI tools can help you identify the most suitable literary agents or publishers for your genre, by analysing submission guidelines and success rates.

Additionally, AI can assist in crafting a compelling query letter, offering suggestions on how to pitch your book effectively to stand out in a crowded market.

By leveraging AI, you can increase your chances of getting noticed by the right people in the publishing industry.

Marketing with AI

Crafting a Compelling Book Blurb: *A well-written book blurb is essential for attracting potential readers.*

AI can help you craft a blurb that highlights the most compelling aspects of your book. You can input a summary of your book, and the AI will generate a blurb that captures the key elements, such as the main conflict, the protagonist's journey, and the emotional stakes. However, it's important to review and refine the AI-generated blurb to ensure it aligns with your vision and resonates with your target audience.

Designing Effective Marketing Strategies: *Marketing is a crucial component of your book's success, and AI can help you design effective strategies tailored to your audience.*

AI tools can analyse market trends, reader demographics, and social media engagement to suggest the best platforms and tactics for promoting your book.

For example, AI might identify specific keywords that are currently trending in your genre, which you can then incorporate into your marketing campaigns.

By using AI to guide your marketing efforts, you can maximise your book's visibility and reach.

Engaging with Your Audience Using AI: *Building a relationship with your readers is vital for long-term success.*

AI can assist in managing your online presence and engaging with your audience through personalised content.

For example, AI can help you automate social media posts, ensuring consistent communication with your followers.

Additionally, AI can analyse reader feedback and reviews to provide insights into what your audience loves about your book and what areas could be improved in future works. This feedback loop allows you to continuously refine your approach and build a loyal readership.

AI Prompts

AI-Generated Writing Prompts

This section offers a diverse collection of AI-generated writing prompts designed to spark your creativity and help you overcome writer's block.

These prompts span a wide range of genres and themes, from science fiction and fantasy to romance and historical fiction.

Each prompt serves as a starting point for short stories, novel chapters, or even full-length projects, providing you with the inspiration needed to explore new ideas and experiment with your writing.

By using these prompts, you can dive into unfamiliar genres, challenge your imagination, and discover innovative ways to incorporate AI into your writing process.

Science Fiction Prompts:

- *Prompt 1:* "In a future where humans have colonized the moon, a mysterious illness starts to spread, causing people to forget their lives on Earth. What happens when the protagonist begins to lose their memories?"

- *Prompt 2:* "A world where everyone is born with a unique superpower, but the powers only activate when they face their greatest fear. The story follows a young person who has lived a fear-free life—until now."

- *Prompt 3:* "After a global blackout, the world's technology is rendered useless. Society must rebuild from scratch, and a small community discovers that the key to survival lies in ancient knowledge long forgotten."

Fantasy Prompts:

- *Prompt 1:* "In a kingdom where the royal family is cursed to live only one day each year, a young prince must find a way to break the curse before his time runs out."

- *Prompt 2:* "A magical forest that changes shape every night, confusing anyone who dares to enter. The protagonist is tasked with navigating the forest to find a lost treasure, but they must first earn the trust of the forest's guardian spirits."

- *Prompt 3:* "A world where people can bind their souls to mythical creatures, gaining their abilities but also sharing their fate. A young warrior binds with a dragon, only to discover the dragon is the last of its kind."

Romance Prompts:

- *Prompt 1:* "A love story set in a world where people can communicate only through dreams. The protagonists meet each other in their dreams, but must find a way to connect in the real world."

- *Prompt 2:* "Two people are fated to fall in love but are always reborn on opposite sides of a war. This time, they decide to break the cycle, but doing so may mean sacrificing their lives."

- *Prompt 3:* "In a small town where everyone knows each other's secrets, a new arrival brings with them a mysterious past. As they grow closer to a local, their secrets threaten to unravel both their lives."

Historical Fiction Prompts:

- *Prompt 1:* "Set during the height of the Roman Empire, a gladiator rises to fame but becomes embroiled in a plot to overthrow the emperor. The story explores their internal conflict between loyalty and freedom."

- *Prompt 2: "During World War II, a spy must navigate the dangerous waters of espionage while maintaining a double life. When their two worlds collide, they must choose between duty and love."*

- *Prompt 3: "In the midst of the French Revolution, a young noblewoman disguises herself as a commoner to escape execution. As she fights for survival, she becomes entangled in the revolution itself, questioning everything she once believed."*

Mystery/Thriller Prompts:

- *Prompt 1: "A detective who can solve any crime—except the one that took their own memory. What happens when they begin investigating their own past?"*

- *Prompt 2: "In a small town, people start receiving anonymous letters revealing their darkest secrets. The letters force them to confront their pasts, but who is behind the revelations, and what do they want?"*

- *Prompt 3: "A high-profile lawyer wakes up in a hotel room covered in blood with no memory of the previous night. They must uncover what happened before the police do—and before they're framed for a crime they didn't commit."*

Adventure Prompts:

- *Prompt 1: "A world where the seasons change every 24 hours, and how one family adapts to the ever-shifting environment."*

- *Prompt 2: "An ancient map leads to a hidden island that doesn't appear on any modern charts. A group of explorers set out to uncover its secrets, but the island is more dangerous than they anticipated."*

- *Prompt 3: "After a plane crash in the Amazon, a group of survivors must navigate the treacherous jungle while being hunted by an unknown predator. Along the way, they discover the jungle hides ancient ruins with secrets worth killing for."*

These AI-generated writing prompts are designed to kickstart your creativity, helping you explore new ideas and directions in your writing.

By experimenting with these prompts, you can break through creative blocks, expand your storytelling skills, and even develop new projects that blend your unique voice with AI-inspired concepts.

Prompts for Collaborative Writing with AI

Collaborative writing with AI offers a unique opportunity to blend your creativity with the AI's ability to generate ideas, suggest plot developments, and refine content. This process of back-and-forth engagement can lead to the creation of stories that are both innovative and reflective of your personal style. Below are several prompts specifically designed to help you explore this collaborative process.

1. Mystery Plot Development

- *Prompt: "Start with a brief outline of a mystery plot. Describe the setting, main character, and initial crime. Let the AI suggest twists, additional suspects, and potential motives. Refine the storyline by selecting the elements that resonate with your vision. Continue this dialogue until you have a fully developed plot with a surprising conclusion."*

- *Example Interaction:*

  ○   *You: "The story begins in a small coastal town where a local fisherman is found dead under mysterious circumstances. The main character, a retired detective, is called in to investigate."*

- AI: "The detective discovers that the fisherman had recently argued with a wealthy landowner over a property dispute. However, clues also suggest the involvement of a secretive local cult. The detective uncovers a hidden journal that might hold the key to the mystery but mysteriously disappears."

- You: "I like the idea of the secretive cult. Let's explore that further. How could the cult be connected to the fisherman's death?"

2. Character Backstory Creation

- *Prompt: "Create a brief profile of a character, including their name, occupation, and one defining trait. Ask the AI to generate a backstory that explains how this trait developed. Use the AI's input to deepen the character's history and motivations, crafting a richer, more complex persona."*

- *Example Interaction:*

  ◦ *You: "The character's name is Elena, a quiet librarian who is fiercely protective of an old, mysterious book collection."*

  ◦ *AI: "Elena inherited the library from her grandmother, who was a renowned historian. Growing up, Elena spent hours in the library, captivated by tales of forgotten lore. Her protective nature stems from a childhood incident where a valuable manuscript was nearly stolen, leaving her with a deep-seated mistrust of outsiders."*

  ◦ *You: "Interesting! Let's expand on the incident—perhaps it involved a close friend who betrayed her. How did that shape her relationships as an adult?"*

3. Dialogue Enhancement

- *Prompt: "Write a rough draft of a dialogue scene between two characters. Ask the AI to suggest ways to make the conversation more engaging or reveal deeper emotions. Revise the dialogue based on the AI's suggestions, aiming for a more natural and impactful exchange."*

- *Example Interaction:*

  ○ *You: "Character A: 'I don't know if I can trust you anymore.' Character B: 'You have to. It's the only way we're going to get through this.'"*

  ○ *AI: "Character A: 'Trust? After what you did? I can't even look at you the same way.' Character B: 'I know I hurt you, but if we don't work together, we'll lose everything.'"*

  ○ *You: "I like the added intensity. Let's continue with Character A expressing doubt but also a reluctant willingness to try."*

4. World-Building Collaboration

- *Prompt: "Outline the basic elements of a fictional world, including its geography, culture, and key conflicts. Let the AI suggest additional world-building details such as societal norms, unique technologies, or historical events. Integrate these ideas to create a rich, immersive setting for your story."*

- *Example Interaction:*

  ○ *You: "The world is a desert planet where water is the most valuable resource. The society is divided between nomadic tribes and wealthy city-dwellers who control the water supply."*

  ○ *AI: "The city-dwellers have developed a complex water purification system that they guard jealously. The nomadic tribes, however, possess ancient knowledge of hidden water sources that the city-dwellers have long forgotten. Tensions rise as the planet's climate becomes even harsher, leading to conflicts over these resources."*

○ *You: "Let's expand on the ancient knowledge—maybe it involves a lost technology or a sacred ritual. How does this influence the power dynamics between the tribes and the city?"*

5. Genre-Mixing Experiment

- *Prompt: "Start with a story concept in your usual genre. Ask the AI to suggest elements from a different genre to incorporate. Experiment with blending these genres, refining the plot, characters, and setting to create a hybrid story that challenges traditional genre boundaries."*

- *Example Interaction:*

  - *You: "The story is a crime thriller about a detective investigating a series of high-profile murders."*

  - *AI: "Consider adding a science fiction twist—the murders are linked to a rogue AI that was once used for military purposes. The detective must navigate a world where technology and crime intersect, and even question their own reliance on AI tools."*

  - *You: "That's an intriguing twist. Let's explore how the rogue AI operates and how it might manipulate both the detective and the evidence to its advantage."*

These prompts are designed to engage you in a creative dialogue with AI, where your input and the AI's suggestions blend to produce unique and innovative story elements. By collaborating with AI in this way, you can push the boundaries of your creativity, experiment with new ideas, and refine your work with a fresh perspective.

Exercises for Improving Writing with AI

This section provides a series of exercises designed to help you improve your writing by using AI tools effectively.

These exercises focus on various aspects of the writing process, including character development, dialogue creation, and scene construction.

Each exercise offers step-by-step instructions on how to use AI to generate content, refine your ideas, and enhance your storytelling.

By engaging in these practical, hands-on activities, you'll be able to apply what you've learned and see tangible improvements in your writing.

1. Developing a Character's Backstory

Objective: To create a rich and consistent backstory for a character using AI.

Instructions:

Begin by writing a brief description of your character, including their appearance, personality traits, and role in the story.

Input this description into an AI tool (such as Sudowrite or GPT-3) and ask it to generate a backstory.

Review the AI-generated backstory, identifying elements that align with your character's role and those that don't.

Refine and edit the backstory, ensuring it adds depth and consistency to the character's development in your story.

Integrate the refined backstory into your manuscript, using it to guide the character's actions and decisions throughout the narrative.

Example:

Input: "Elena is a 35-year-old librarian, introverted and meticulous, with a passion for preserving ancient books."

AI Output: "Elena grew up in a small town, where her grandmother, the town's only historian, taught her the value of preserving knowledge. After a fire destroyed her childhood home and its library, Elena dedicated her life to protecting rare books, driven by the memory of the lost history."

Refinement: Adjust the backstory to include a specific event in Elena's adulthood that rekindles her fears, motivating her actions in the story.

2. Enhancing Dialogue

Objective: To create natural, engaging dialogue that reveals character and advances the plot.

Instructions:

Write a rough draft of a dialogue scene between two or more characters.

Input this draft into an AI tool and request suggestions for improving the dialogue, focusing on making it more natural or impactful.

Compare the AI's suggestions with your original draft, identifying areas where the AI's input enhances the conversation's flow or depth.

Revise the dialogue, incorporating the best elements from both the AI's suggestions and your original work.

Test the revised dialogue by reading it aloud to ensure it sounds authentic and meets the scene's goals.

Example:

Original Dialogue: "I'm not sure if we should trust him." "We don't have a choice; we need his help."

AI Suggestion: "I don't know if I can trust him after what he did." "Do we have a choice? Without him, we're stuck."

Refinement: Combine the suggestions to deepen the characters' relationship and increase the tension in the scene.

3. Constructing a Scene

Objective: To build a compelling scene that immerses readers in the setting and drives the plot forward.

Instructions:

Outline the basic elements of a scene, including the setting, characters, and main action.

Input this outline into an AI tool, asking it to expand on the scene with sensory details, background information, and character interactions.

Review the AI-generated content, selecting the details and descriptions that best enhance your original vision.

Integrate these details into your scene, ensuring that they contribute to the overall mood and progression of the plot.

Revise the scene to maintain consistency with the rest of your narrative and to refine any AI-generated content that needs further polishing.

Example:

Outline: "A stormy night. The protagonist arrives at an old mansion to confront the antagonist. Tension is high."

AI Output: "Lightning flashes across the sky, casting eerie shadows on the mansion's stone walls. The protagonist's heart races as they approach the massive oak doors, which creak ominously in the wind. Inside, the faint glow of a fireplace flickers, but the air is thick with the smell of damp wood and something more sinister."

Refinement: Use the AI's atmospheric details to heighten the tension in the confrontation scene.

4. Exploring Different Writing Styles

Objective: To experiment with different writing styles and voices to find the best fit for your narrative.

Instructions:

Choose a passage from your current writing project.

Input the passage into an AI tool and ask it to rewrite the passage in different styles (e.g., more formal, conversational, poetic, or terse).

Review the different versions generated by the AI, noting how each style changes the tone and impact of the passage.

Select the style that best aligns with the overall voice of your story or that introduces a new, effective way of telling the story.

Incorporate elements of this style into your passage and consider applying it more broadly in your manuscript.

Example:

Original Passage: "The city was quiet at night, with only the occasional car passing by."

AI Styles:

Formal: "The city lay in tranquil silence as night enveloped it, interrupted only by the infrequent hum of a solitary automobile."

Conversational: "The city was pretty quiet, except for a car driving by now and then."

Poetic: "The city slumbered under a blanket of night, its stillness broken only by the fleeting whisper of a car's engine."

Refinement: Choose the style that best suits the mood and pace of your story, and revise the passage accordingly.

5. Generating Plot Twists

Objective: To create unexpected plot twists that keep readers engaged and surprised.

Instructions:

Outline the main events of your story up to a critical turning point.

Input this outline into an AI tool and request suggestions for potential plot twists that could alter the direction of the story.

Evaluate the AI-generated twists, considering how each one could add depth, complexity, or suspense to your narrative.

Select or modify a twist that fits well with your characters and plot, ensuring it aligns with the story's overall theme.

Integrate the twist into your story, adjusting the subsequent events and character reactions to reflect the new direction.

Example:

Outline: "The protagonist believes they have uncovered the identity of the villain, but just as they are about to confront them, something unexpected happens."

AI Plot Twist: "The villain reveals they were manipulated by a higher power all along, turning the protagonist's ally into the real threat."

Refinement: Decide how this twist impacts the protagonist's journey and adjust the plot to accommodate this new revelation.

These exercises are designed to be practical and hands-on, allowing you to apply AI tools to your writing process in meaningful ways.

By practicing these exercises, you'll develop a better understanding of how AI can enhance your storytelling, improve your writing skills, and make your creative process more dynamic and innovative.

I hope you enjoyed reading this, as much as I enjoyed putting it together, get out there today and have fun creating your next novel! Do look at the appendices for lots of references to useful tools and terms

Appendix

Resources and Tools

In this appendix, you'll find a detailed list of AI tools that can assist you at every stage of the writing process.

Whether you're looking for a tool to help brainstorm ideas, generate content, or polish your prose, this list includes options that cater to various needs.

By exploring these resources, you can expand your toolkit and discover new ways to enhance your writing with AI.

Comprehensive List of AI Writing Tools:

Here's a comprehensive list of AI writing tools, including their URLs:

ChatGPT

OpenAi's ChatGPT

    Website:https://chatgpt.com/

Grammarly*An AI-powered writing assistant that helps with grammar, punctuation, style, and tone.*

Website: https://www.grammarly.com/

Hemingway Editor*A tool that focuses on making your writing clear and concise by highlighting complex sentences and suggesting simpler alternatives.*

Website: https://hemingwayapp.com/

ProWritingAid*A comprehensive writing assistant that checks grammar, style, and consistency while offering in-depth reports to improve your writing.*

Website: https://prowritingaid.com/

Sudowrite*An AI tool designed specifically for creative writers to help generate ideas, complete sentences, and improve narratives.*

Website: https://www.sudowrite.com/

Jasper (formerly Jarvis)*An AI content generator that helps with copywriting, blog posts, and marketing content.*

Website: https://www.jasper.ai/

Writesonic*An AI writer that generates content for ads, blog posts, landing pages, and more.*

Website: https://writesonic.com/

Copy.ai An AI tool designed to assist with creating marketing copy, product descriptions, and more.

Website: https://www.copy.ai/

WordtuneA writing assistant that helps rewrite sentences to improve clarity, fluency, and tone.

Website: https://www.wordtune.com/

QuillBotAn AI-powered paraphrasing tool that helps rephrase sentences while retaining the original meaning.

Website: https://quillbot.com/

AI DungeonA text-based adventure game powered by AI that allows you to create and explore stories interactively.

Website: https://play.aidungeon.io/

RytrAn AI writing tool that helps generate high-quality content for blogs, emails, social media, and more.

Website: https://rytr.me/

INK EditorA writing tool that optimizes content for SEO while providing AI-powered suggestions.

Website: https://inkforall.com/

TextioAn augmented writing platform that helps improve the tone and effectiveness of job descriptions and other business writing.

Website: https://textio.com/

Linguix A writing assistant focused on improving grammar, style, and clarity, with additional tools for non-native English speakers.

Website: https://linguix.com/

Scrivener A popular writing software for long-form content, which integrates with AI tools to help organise and enhance the writing process.

Website: https://www.literatureandlatte.com/scrivener/overview

ShortlyAI An AI writing tool that helps generate and expand on text, particularly for long-form content like articles and stories.

Website: https://www.shortlyai.com/

WriteCream An AI-powered tool that helps create personalised marketing emails, blog posts, and ad copy.

Website: https://www.writecream.com/

Narrative Device A tool that uses AI to help writers plan and structure their stories by analysing narrative elements.

Website: https://www.narrativedevice.com/

StoryLab.ai An AI tool designed to help you brainstorm story ideas, write compelling headlines, and create engaging narratives.

Website: https://www.storylab.ai/

Peppertype.ai An AI-powered writing tool that generates high-quality content for blogs, social media, and more.

Website: https://www.peppertype.ai/

These tools vary in their specific applications and target users, from creative writing and content generation to grammar checking and SEO optimisation, offering a broad range of support for different writing needs.

Writing and Editing Software:

When it comes to writing and editing, traditional software like word processors and specialised writing platforms can be effectively paired with AI tools to enhance your workflow from drafting to final edits. Here's a look at some recommended writing and editing software and how they can work in tandem with AI tools:

1. Microsoft Word

Overview: Microsoft Word is one of the most widely used word processors, offering robust features for drafting, editing, and formatting documents. It also supports various integrations with AI tools.

AI Integration: Microsoft Word integrates with AI-driven tools like Grammarly, ProWritingAid, and Wordtune, allowing you to check grammar, style, and tone directly within the document. Additionally, Microsoft Editor, built into Word, provides AI-powered writing suggestions.

Use Case: Use Word for drafting and editing your manuscript, with AI tools providing real-time feedback and suggestions to refine your content.

Website: https://www.microsoft.com/en-us/microsoft-365/word

2. Google Docs

Overview: Google Docs is a cloud-based word processor that allows for real-time collaboration. Its flexibility and ease of use make it a popular choice for writers.

AI Integration: Google Docs can be enhanced with AI tools like Grammarly, which offers a browser extension that integrates seamlessly. Google's own AI-driven Smart Compose and spelling suggestions help streamline the writing process.

Use Case: Leverage Google Docs for collaborative projects, with AI tools helping to maintain consistency and clarity across different contributors.

Website: https://docs.google.com/

3. Scrivener

Overview: Scrivener is a powerful tool designed for long-form writing projects such as novels, screenplays, and research papers. It allows you to organize your writing into sections, scenes, and chapters.

AI Integration: While Scrivener itself doesn't have built-in AI tools, you can use AI tools like Sudowrite or Jasper alongside it. Draft content in Scrivener, then use AI tools to generate ideas, expand on sections, or refine specific parts of your manuscript.

Use Case: Use Scrivener to structure and organize your project, and turn to AI tools for creative assistance and content generation when needed.

Website: https://www.literatureandlatte.com/scrivener/overview

4. Ulysses

Overview: Ulysses is a writing app designed for authors, bloggers, and anyone who needs a focused writing environment. It offers a clean interface with tools for organising and managing writing projects.

AI Integration: Ulysses can be paired with AI tools like Grammarly or Hemingway by exporting text to these platforms for editing and refinement. You can also use AI-based services like ShortlyAI to brainstorm ideas before importing them into Ulysses.

Use Case: Write and organize your content in Ulysses, then export to AI-powered tools for enhanced editing and feedback.

Website: https://ulysses.app/

5. Final Draft

Overview: Final Draft is a leading screenwriting software that provides industry-standard formatting and tools tailored for scriptwriting.

AI Integration: While Final Draft is focused on scriptwriting, you can use AI tools like Grammarly for grammar and style checks or StoryLab.ai for generating plot ideas and character development suggestions before importing them into Final Draft.

Use Case: Write and format your screenplay in Final Draft, with AI tools offering creative input and editing suggestions during the writing process.

Website: https://www.finaldraft.com/

How These Programs Work with AI Tools:

Drafting: Start with your preferred word processor (Microsoft Word or Google Docs) or specialised software (Scrivener or Ulysses) to draft your content.

Use AI tools like ChatGPT to brainstorm ideas, generate text, or receive real-time writing suggestions to enhance your initial drafts.

Editing: Once your draft is complete, use AI-powered plugins like Grammarly or ProWritingAid integrated within these platforms to refine grammar, style, and clarity. These AI tools can also help with consistency checks, ensuring that your narrative voice remains strong and cohesive.

Final Edits: *For specialised writing tasks, like scriptwriting in Final Draft or long-form projects in Scrivener, AI tools can assist with polishing the final manuscript, suggesting improvements, and helping to ensure that the final product is of the highest quality.*

By combining traditional writing software with AI tools, you can create a streamlined, efficient workflow that enhances both the creative and technical aspects of your writing, ultimately leading to a more polished and professional final product.

Educational Resources and Tutorials

To help you get the most out of your AI tools, this section provides a curated list of educational resources and tutorials.

These resources range from online courses and video tutorials to blog posts and guides, all designed to help you understand and effectively use AI in your writing.

Whether you're just beginning your journey with AI or looking to deepen your expertise, these materials offer valuable insights and practical, step-by-step guidance.

1. Online Courses

Coursera: AI for Everyone

Description: This course, taught by Andrew Ng, provides a broad overview of AI concepts, making it accessible to non-technical users. It's ideal for understanding the basics of AI and its applications in various fields, including writing.

Link: AI for Everyone on Coursera

Udemy: The Complete AI Writing Assistant with GPT-3

Description: A hands-on course that teaches you how to use GPT-3, one of the most powerful AI models, for writing tasks. It covers everything from generating text to enhancing creative writing with AI.

Link: The Complete AI Writing Assistant on Udemy

2. Video Tutorials

YouTube: Grammarly Tutorials

Description: Grammarly's official YouTube channel offers a series of tutorials on how to use their AI-powered writing assistant effectively, covering both basic and advanced features.

Link: Grammarly on YouTube

YouTube: Writing with AI (by Sudowrite)

Description: Sudowrite's channel provides tutorials and demos on how to use their AI tool for creative writing, focusing on generating ideas, improving narratives, and more.

Link: Sudowrite on YouTube

AI Dungeon Tutorials

Description: Learn how to create interactive stories using AI Dungeon, with step-by-step guides and examples of how to harness the AI's narrative capabilities.

Link: AI Dungeon on YouTube

3. Blog Posts and Guides

OpenAI Blog

Description: The OpenAI blog provides in-depth articles and guides on using AI for various applications, including writing. It's a great resource for staying updated on the latest advancements and learning new techniques.

Link: OpenAI Blog

ProWritingAid Blog

Description: The ProWritingAid blog offers tips, tutorials, and writing advice, with a focus on using their AI tool to enhance your writing. It's useful for learning how to integrate AI into your editing process.

Link: ProWritingAid Blog

Writing Cooperative: How to Use AI to Write Better

Description: This article explores practical ways to incorporate AI into your writing routine, offering tips and examples for improving your writing with AI assistance.

Link: How to Use AI to Write Better on Medium

By taking advantage of these educational resources and tutorials, you can improve your skills and become more confident in integrating AI into your writing process. These materials not only help you understand the technical aspects of AI tools but also guide you in applying them creatively, ensuring that you can leverage AI to enhance every stage of your writing journey.

Glossary of AI and Writing Terms

Understanding Key Terminology:

As you navigate the world of AI-assisted writing, it's crucial to understand both the technical jargon of AI and the specialized terms of the writing industry. This glossary provides clear and concise definitions of key terms, helping you effectively use AI tools and communicate your needs when collaborating with others.

AI-Related Terms:

- ***Artificial Intelligence (AI):*** *The field of computer science focused on creating systems capable of performing tasks that typically require human intelligence, such as learning, reasoning, problem-solving, and understanding natural language.*

- ***Machine Learning (ML):*** *A subset of AI where computer algorithms are designed to learn from data and improve their performance over time without being explicitly programmed for each task.*

- ***Natural Language Processing (NLP):*** *A branch of AI that focuses on enabling computers to understand, interpret, and generate human language. NLP powers tools like chatbots, translation services, and AI writing assistants.*

- ***Neural Network:*** *A computational model inspired by the human brain, consisting of interconnected nodes (neurons) that process information and learn from data. Neural networks are the foundation of deep learning, which drives many advanced AI applications.*

- ***Transformer Models:*** *A type of neural network architecture particularly effective for NLP tasks. Transformer models, like GPT (Generative Pre-trained Transformer), are designed to understand and generate text by considering the context of words in relation to each other.*

- ***Deep Learning:*** *A subset of machine learning that involves neural networks with many layers (deep neural networks). Deep learning models can analyze* complex patterns in large datasets, making them highly effective for tasks like image recognition and natural language processing.

- **GPT (Generative Pre-trained Transformer):** *A type of transformer model developed by OpenAI that generates human-like text. GPT models are pre-trained on vast amounts of text data and can generate content based on user prompts, making them powerful tools for writing assistance.*

- **Algorithm:** *A set of rules or instructions given to an AI system to help it learn and make decisions. In writing tools, algorithms might help generate text, correct grammar, or suggest stylistic improvements.*

Writing-Specific Terms:

- **Plot Arc:** *The structured development of a story's plot, usually involving a beginning, middle, and end, with key events that build tension and lead to a resolution.*

- **Character Development:** *The process of creating and evolving characters in a story, ensuring they have depth, motivations, and a dynamic presence that drives the narrative forward.*

- **Theme:** *The underlying message or central idea explored in a story. Themes often reflect universal human experiences, such as love, betrayal, or redemption.*

- **Motif:** *A recurring element, such as an image, symbol, or phrase, that reinforces the theme or central ideas of a narrative.*

- **Narrative Voice:** *The perspective from which a story is told, including the tone, style, and personality of the narrator. The narrative voice significantly influences how the story is perceived by readers.*

- **Dialogue:** *The written conversation between characters in a story. Effective dialogue advances the plot, reveals character traits, and enhances the realism of the narrative.*

- **Genre:**A category of literature defined by similarities in form, style, or content. Common genres include fantasy, science fiction, romance, and mystery.

- **Protagonist:**The main character in a story, often facing challenges that drive the plot forward. The protagonist's journey is typically central to the narrative.

- **Antagonist:**A character, group, or force that opposes the protagonist, creating conflict in the story.

- **Manuscript:**The complete, written version of a work, such as a novel, screenplay, or non-fiction book, often submitted to publishers or editors for consideration.

Simplifying Complex AI Concepts:

Some AI concepts can be complex, especially if you're new to the field. This glossary breaks down these ideas into easy-to-understand explanations, linking them directly to your writing process.

- **Transformer Models:**Explained as advanced AI structures designed to understand the context of words and generate human-like text, making them essential for tools that help you draft and refine your writing.

- **Neural Networks:**Described as models that mimic how the human brain processes information, allowing AI to learn and recognize patterns, such as common writing styles or the structure of a well-crafted sentence.

By familiarising yourself with these terms, you'll be better equipped to use AI tools effectively, understand how they can enhance your writing, and communicate your needs clearly when seeking assistance or collaborating with others. This knowledge empowers you to integrate AI seamlessly into your creative process, ensuring that technology complements rather than complicates your writing journey.